D1303397

10/07

THIS BOOK BELONGS TO:

. . . .

tiger tales
an imprint of ME Media, LLC
202 Old Ridgefield Road, Wilton, CT 06897
First published in the United States 2006
Originally published in Great Britain 2006
by Andersen Press Ltd
Text and illustrations copyright ©2006 Michael Foreman
CIP Data is available
ISBN-10: 1-58925-401-5
ISBN-13: 978-1-58925-401-5
Printed in Singapore

Norman's Ark

by Michael Foreman

tiger tales

Norman is a good little boy who never tells a lie.
Honest.
It's just that some people don't believe him.
People like his mom and dad, for instance.

Take last summer. Norman and his parents
vacationed at a safari park. They stayed in
huts, except the roofs weren't real straw.
They were plastic.

But the animals were real. Norman liked
the animals.

Norman had his very own hut. At night,
he liked to get into bed early and watch TV.
One night, there was a terrible storm.
Rain pounded on the plastic straw roof and
thunder rolled.

Suddenly, Norman heard a noise at the door. He peeped out of the window and saw a pair of anteaters huddled on his porch.

Then a pair of pandas appeared, followed by two aardvarks. They all squished together, taking cover from the rain.

"Luckily, they're all small," Norman said.

Then some kangaroos came hopping out of the darkness. They pushed on Norman's door with their big feet and long tails until Norman could see it begin to bulge.

None of the animals seemed dangerous, so Norman opened the door...

and they all tumbled in!

But then the really big animals began to show up.
The hippos were first. They had to hold their
breath to squeeze through the door.

The first rhinoceros managed to get his big horned head into the room, but then he got stuck, so the second rhinoceros had to stay outside…with the elephants.

Smaller arrivals, like the koalas, tapirs, and porcupines, scrambled through the rhino's legs.

The prickly quills of the porcupines tickled the rhino's tummy and made him giggle, and the hyenas couldn't stop laughing.

The orangutans and baboons made
themselves at home on the sofa.

The sloths went straight to bed ... *under* the bed, that is. The bed was already full of bears and buffalo.

The ostriches and emus had a squabble, the giraffes and grumpy camels didn't see eye to eye, and...

the skunks made a terrible smell in the bathroom.
But, Norman decided, all things considered,
the evening was going well.

Norman was relieved that the jammed
rhino in the doorway kept the lions, leopards,
and tigers from getting in.

When the rain stopped at last, the animals said their goodbyes and thank yous to Norman and wandered off into the night, two by two.

Norman had tried to clean up before his parents came in, but it was a mammoth job.

"Where's a good mammoth when you need one?" he asked.

"What's been going on here, Norman?" exclaimed his mother, with a gasp. "How did you make such a mess?"

"I had a little help," said Norman, who always told the truth.

"What help?" demanded his dad.

"You don't know anyone here!"

"There were pandas and porcupines, kangaroos and koalas, rhinos, raccoons and reindeer, ostriches and emus, bears and buffalo, and others I can't remember.

Oh, and there may still be bats in the bathroom, but I didn't make the smell in there. It was the skunks."

"Is that all?" shouted his father.

"There were lions and tigers and leopards, but they didn't come in," said Norman.

"Well, we don't believe a word of it," his mom said. "We're leaving in the morning, and when we get home we don't want to hear any more of these silly fibs of yours, Norman."

The next morning, when Norman and his parents were leaving the safari park, the animals lined up, two by two, and waved.

"Bye, Norman!" they shouted. "Thanks for last night! And thanks for your address. We'll come and visit soon."

"Norman!" said his dad. "I hope you didn't give them our real address."

"But Dad," said Norman, "I couldn't tell a lie."